The Quest for Your Life Purpose

A Guide to Finding Your Life Path

The Quest for Your Life Purpose

A Guide to Finding Your Life Path

Marsha Ferrick Heiden, PhD., BCC

Author

Marie Billings Dalton

Artist

The Quest for Your Life Purpose
A Guide to Finding Your Life Path

Written by *Marsha Ferrick Heiden, PhD., BCC*
Art by *Marie Billings Dalton*

Marsha Ferrick Heiden, PhD, BCC
Amara Quest, Inc.
8322 State Route 305
Garrettsville, OH 44231

http://www.amaraquest.com

To:

Maureen

Contents

The Journey Begins

Your Name

Date

What is a Quest?

A quest is a journey to find something. In this quest it is a journey to find your life purpose. It is a journey to find a deeper connection to yourself and to others. It is a journey of growth, realization, and creation. Ultimately it is a quest to live fully engaged with life in a way that allows you to be your most awesome self! On your journey, what do you hope to find?

My, I Want to Do List!

To find your life purpose let's start with a list of at least 100 things you **want** to achieve or do in your lifetime (not daily activities). Be bold, do not hesitate, let your creativity, and spontaneity unfold without any judgments or barriers about the items you write down on your list. Write the list quickly, putting the ideas unto paper as soon as they come into your mind. Do not evaluate them (that can be done later)! Have fun, be excited! Continue to add to this list as new ideas come to mind! You will revisit this list time and time again as you work on your quest and throughout your lifetime. Don't worry if you cannot think of 100 items on your first attempt just keep going and more ideas will unfold as you move through this process. If you can think of more than 100 just keep listing them!

Be Curious

Consider your interests, ask yourself questions. What non-fiction books do you enjoy reading? What type of documentaries do you watch? What newspapers or magazine articles do you choose to read? What do you enjoy learning about?

The Riches of Curiosity

What we are naturally curious about is often what we are passionate about in life. As you ponder the things you wrote you were curious about consider that within your curiosity may lie clues about professions in which you would thrive. We often seek out things we naturally enjoy the most. Reflect on the thing you were curious about. Make a list of the obvious things you are interested in, then reflect on the deeper connections your interests may have with each other. What do they have in common? Where are they different? What draws you to them? What excites you about them?

Change

What do you WANT to change? What societal issues anger you? What news angers you the most? What do you WANT to change in your life, community, or in the world for the benefit of others?

Elixor of Change

We are strongly moved by the things that matter the most to us. The things that are closest to our hearts. What is close to your heart? Write about why you are so passionately moved by the things that you wrote about above? Why is changing these things important to you?

Love To Do

Make a list of things you love to do. List things that you love to do now or that you have loved to do in the past. Make the list as big as you can.

The Message of Love

The things we love to do tell us a great deal about ourselves. They point to our values, our goals, and the kind of life we want to live. What themes show up in your list? What insights did you have?

Success

What would you do if you could not fail? Whatever you decide to do you will succeed at it, there is no limit. If there is no fear of failure, what would you do?

The Gift of Success

Answered honestly the previous question takes you beyond your normal self-imposed limitations and transports you to a place where you live as your truly authentic and awesome self. Consider what it would be like to walk in the world as your awesome self without limitations. Write down how you would be different in the world. What new habits would you create to accomplish this life?

Abundance

What would you do if you had unlimited resources? Often we limit our thinking because we think in terms of the scarcity of money. If you did not have any limits due to money, what would you dedicate yourself to?

The Goodness of Abundance

Often we associate money with bad things such as greed, scarcity or as an obstacle to happiness. Money is none of those things. Money is green. It is a form of currency for trade. Having an abundance of money is a resource that can be used to grow the life you want. Consider how you may be giving yourself and the world mixed messages about money. How are you using the scarcity of money as an excuse or obstacle to getting to where you want to be with your life? How could you change your focus about money to benefit you not detract from you?

Eulogy

You live to a ripe old age living the life you want. You die a quick and peaceful death. Picture your funeral and how everybody close to you is there. What would you like each of these people to say about you and your life? What would you like to hear at your funeral? What kind of a colleague, friend and family member were you? What characteristics would you like them to have seen that they can attribute to you? What contributions and achievements would you have completed that you would have wanted them to remember? Look carefully at each of the people at your funeral, what difference would you like to have made in their lives?

Insight of an Eulogy

Looking at what you would like to hear at your funeral, what have you learned about your values? What have you discovered about what you want your life to be?

Time Flies

What are the things you currently enjoy doing? What things are you doing when time just flies by? Think about recreational and productive activities that you become fully immersed in and lose track of time. List them.

The Well of Flight

Look closely at the things you do when time flies, or you lose track of time. These are the times you are engaged, and participating fully with all of yourself, present to only each moment that passes. Why do you become fully integrated with yourself during these life events? What transforms you in those moments?

Empowering

When have you been the most empowered? What activities or tasks were you doing when you felt empowered? What were you doing when you felt the happiest, most productive and eager to do what you were doing whether it was at home, school, work, or play?

The Brilliance of Empowerment

When you are empowered you feel energized, and you feel excited. You become your best you bringing together all that makes you, you at your very best. You become alive and you discover yourself to be a greater person than you ever dreamed yourself to be. Describe how you feel when doing the things that make you feel empowered. How do you feel different when you are empowered? How do you manifest those feelings? Consider your stance, your internal physiology. How are you different?

The Brilliance of Empowerment

Significance

What have you accomplished in your life that you would most like to be acknowledged for to date in your life?   What big or small accomplishments are you the proudest of for yourself?

The Essence of Significance

Significance comes in many forms. For most of us it is what matters most. What matters the most to you? What can you learn from understanding what matters most to you?

Wish Upon a Star

If you had only one wish that would be granted, what would it be?   Ponder this for a moment before you write it down and then explain why you chose to make that single wish.

The Generosity of Wishes

Now that you wished upon your star for yourself. Think of five or more people for whom you could make a wish, include strangers if you would like to do so. When you are done note any common themes you see that run through them. What are they?

Reinvent Yourself

If you could live anyone's life, whose would it be? Who are the people past or present that you admire? Why?

What is there about these people that appeals to you? Is it something about their achievements, lifestyle or other aspects of life that you find desirable?

Inspiration

What ideas are you most inspired by? Why? The ideas can be about life, career, society or anything that is inspiring to you. Inspiration can come from anywhere or anything. What inspires you? In what way? And why?

The Importance of Inspiration

Inspiration keeps our creating fresh. It excites and motivates us. How does inspiration move you to improve your life?

The Company You Keep

What kind of people would you like to be surrounded by in terms of lifestyle, occupation, wealth, or interests? With whom would you like to surround yourself?

Reflections on Your Company

It is said that you become like the company you keep. If so, how would you change the company you keep?

Responsibility

Are you a victim or an owner? Do you take responsibility for what is happening to you? What kind of person are you? Where are you with your life right now? Do you believe you are the reason for the way your life is right now? Do you blame others for the way your life is right now? Can you create your own future? What needs to change within you?

The Freedom of Responsibility

Only you can change your future and create the life you want to live, no one else. If you blamed others and shifted the responsibility away from yourself list the ways in which you can own your life and the outcomes that occur in it? Consider all areas of your life, where do you tend to blame others and not take ownership of your life?

Identifying Your Life Purpose

Reread what you have written in the previous exercise. What patterns and themes run through your writing including your "My, I Want to Do List"? Make a list of these patterns and themes. Next, simplify them into a cohesive one to three sentence life purpose statement. Keep it broad in what you can encompass in terms of your life and work, but be specific in terms of your life purpose. Take your time. You may rewrite this several times. Over time your purpose may change, so revisit it periodically to make sure it continues to fit for you. Modify or change it as is appropriate. Use action oriented words in your life purpose statement. "My life purpose is...", "I will... instead of I want to or I hope to..." For example, "My purpose for this quest is for the owner of this workbook to create and connect with a clear life purpose, an essential step in the quest for the awesome life she wants to live."

For additional titles visit
www.amaraquest.com